SPORTING LEGENDS

Jillian Powell

orial consultants: Cliff Moon,
aine Petersen and Frances Ridley

Helping Everyone Achieve

nasen
NASEN House, 4/5 Amber Business Village, Amber Close,
Amington, Tamworth, Staffordshire B77 4RP

Rising Stars UK Ltd.
22 Grafton Street, London W1S 4EX
www.risingstars-uk.com

Every effort has been made to trace copyright holders and obtain their permission for use of copyright material. The publisher will gladly receive information enabling them to rectify any error or omission in subsequent editions.
All facts are correct at time of going to press.

Published 2007

Cover design: Button plc
Cover image: Alamy
Text design and typesetting: Andy Wilson
Publisher: Gill Budgell
Project management and editorial: Lesley Densham
Editing: Clare Robertson
Editorial consultants: Cliff Moon, Lorraine Petersen and Frances Ridley
Illustrations: Moreno Chiacchiera: pages 18–19, 28–29, 36–37
Photos: Alamy: pages 4–5, 6, 7, 8, 9, 11, 12, 13, 15, 16, 20–21, 30, 31, 39, 41, 43
Corbis: pages 17, 22, 24–25, 35, 40, 43
Empics: pages 8, 32–33, 34
Getty Images: pages 10, 23, 26–27, 31, 39, 42
TopFoto: pages 14, 38

This book should not be used as a guide to the sports shown in it.
The publisher accepts no responsibility for any harm which might result from taking part in these sports.

British Library Cataloguing in Publication Data.
A CIP record for this book is available from the British Library.

ISBN: 978-1-84680-187-7

Printed by Craft Print International Limited, Singapore

Contents

Legends of sport

They are the best in their sport.

They break records. They win cups and medals.

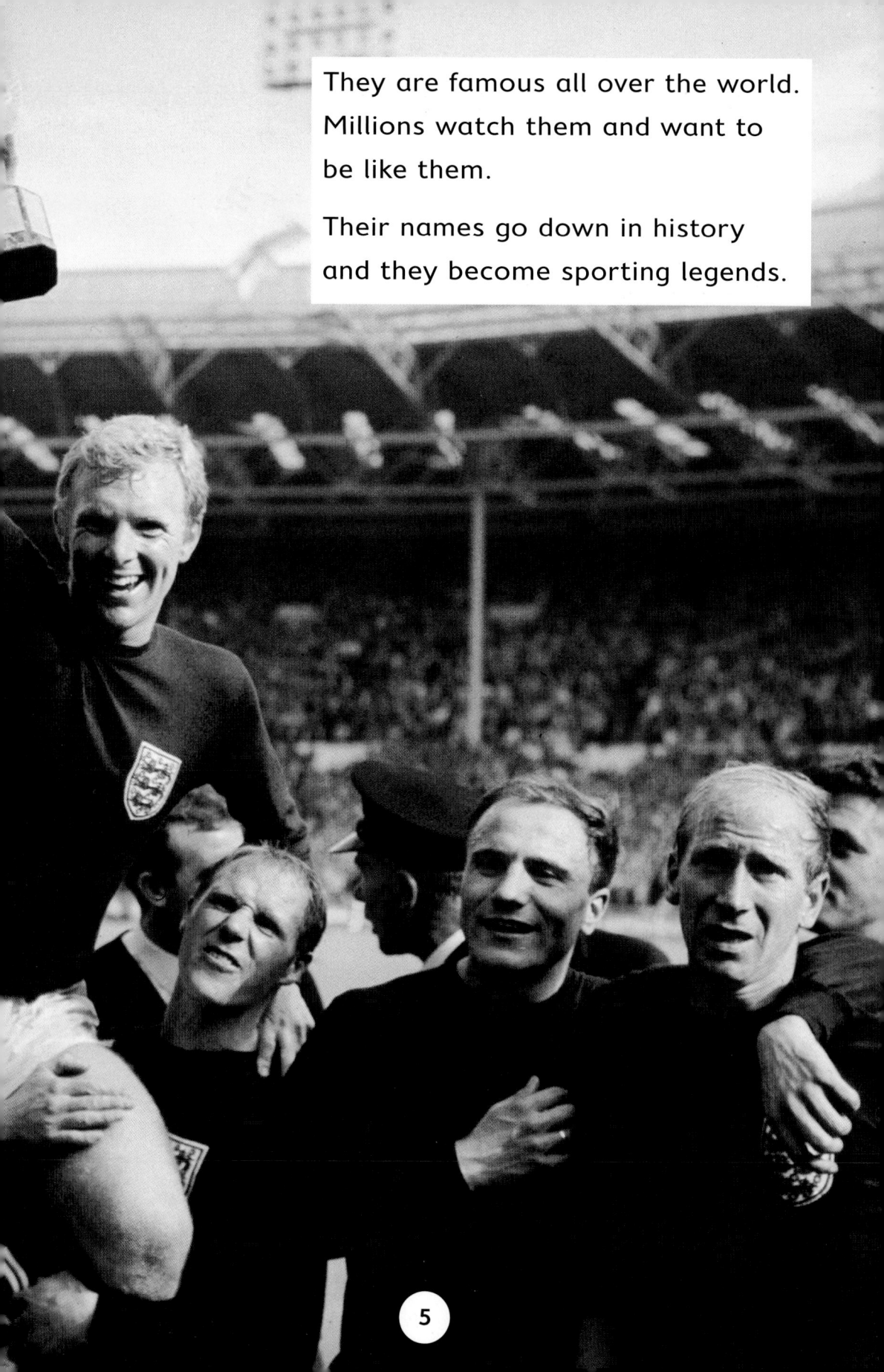

They are famous all over the world.
Millions watch them and want to
be like them.

Their names go down in history
and they become sporting legends.

Great names from the past

Every sport has its legends.

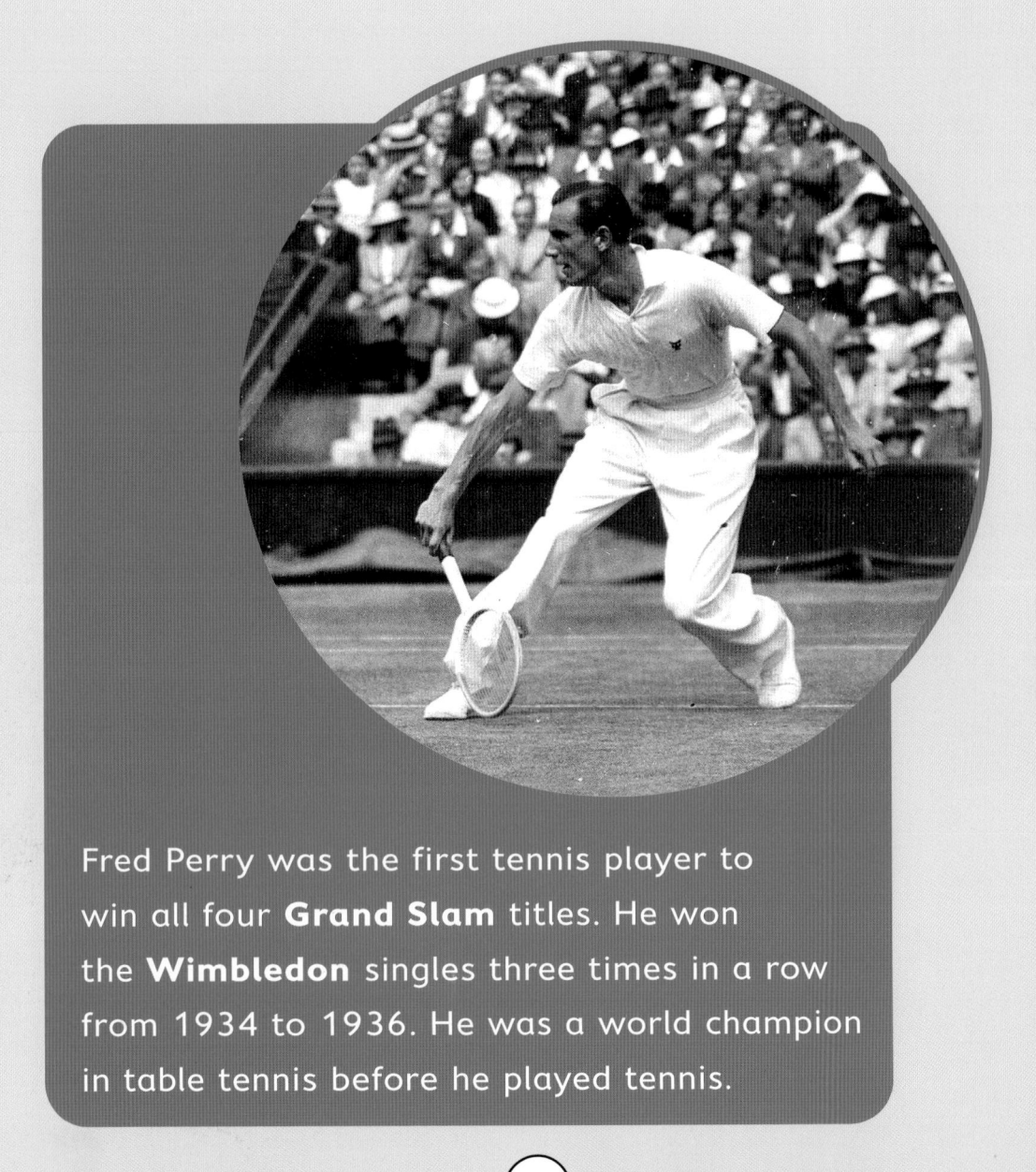

Fred Perry was the first tennis player to win all four **Grand Slam** titles. He won the **Wimbledon** singles three times in a row from 1934 to 1936. He was a world champion in table tennis before he played tennis.

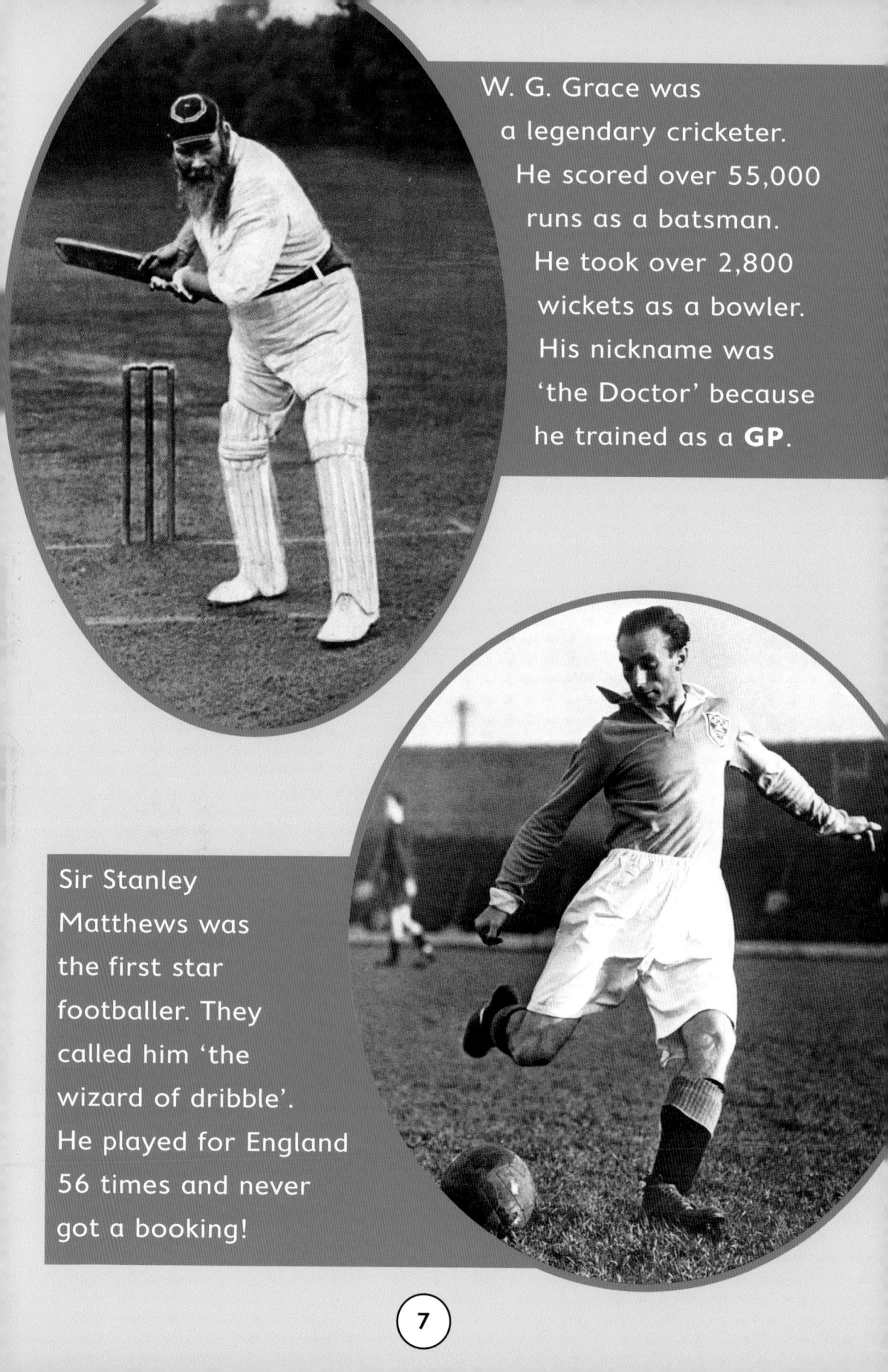

W. G. Grace was a legendary cricketer. He scored over 55,000 runs as a batsman. He took over 2,800 wickets as a bowler. His nickname was 'the Doctor' because he trained as a **GP**.

Sir Stanley Matthews was the first star footballer. They called him 'the wizard of dribble'. He played for England 56 times and never got a booking!

Record-breakers

Some sports stars are remembered as record-breakers.

Jesse Owens won four gold medals at the Berlin **Olympics** in 1936.

He broke Olympic and world records in long jump and three different running events.

Sir Roger Bannister was the first man to run a mile in under four minutes. He set a record of three minutes 59 seconds in Oxford in 1954.

Bob Beamon set a new world long jump record in 1968.
He jumped over 8.8 metres at the Olympic games in Mexico.

More record-breakers		
Legend	Sport	Record
Steve Redgrave	rowing	5 Olympic golds
Martina Navratilova	tennis	9 **Wimbledon** singles titles
Mark Spitz	swimming	7 Olympic golds
Frankie Dettori	horseracing	7 races at Ascot
Michael Schumacher	**Formula One**	7 championships

Football legends

Some footballers become legends for all time.
Their names are famous around the world.

Pelé

Pelé was 17 when his team Brazil won
the World Cup in 1958. He starred in three
World Cup winning squads and his career
lasted 20 years.

Pelé scored over
1,200 goals for his club
Santos. In 2000, he
was named **FIFA**'s
Player of the Century.

Key teams

Santos, New York Cosmos
Brazil: 92 **caps** 77 goals

Diego Maradona

Diego Maradona was the son of
a poor factory worker. He was one
of the best players of the 20th
century. He first played for Argentina
against Hungary when he was 16.

Key teams	
Napoli	
Argentina: 91 caps 34 goals	

George Best

George Best was spotted by a football **scout** when he was at school. He first played for Manchester United when he was 17. He became world famous for his amazing skill. His team won the League Championship in 1965 and 1967 and the European Cup in 1968.

Key teams

Manchester United, Fulham

Northern Ireland: 37 **caps** 9 goals

David Beckham

David Beckham is one of the most famous footballers of all time. He signed for Manchester United in 1991 when he was 16. He first played for England in 1996 and was captain from 2000 to 2006.

Key teams

Manchester United, Real Madrid, LA Galaxy

England: 94 caps 17 goals

1966 World Cup winners

On the 30th of July, 1966, England won the World Cup.

A crowd of 93,000 saw them win at Wembley.

Four hundred million people watched the match on television worldwide.

Geoff Hurst scored a **hat trick**.
He was the first person to do this
in a World Cup final. He scored
his third goal in the final moments
of extra time.
Fans were
already running
onto the pitch.

The television
reporter said
the famous
words:

They think
it's all over …
… it is now!

ENGLAND 3 GERMANY W. 2

England beat West Germany 4–2.
Their captain was Bobby Moore.

It was the first time they had won
since the World Cup began in 1930.

Muhammad Ali

Muhammad Ali is the greatest boxer of
all time.

Ali was born Cassius Clay in Kentucky,
USA in 1942. He changed his name
when he became a Muslim in 1975.

Ali was famous for his light, dancing
style and his **wit**.

Ali became World Heavyweight Champion and a gold medal winner at the **Olympics**.

He was the first man to win the heavyweight title three times.

He was called 'The King of the Ring'.

Boxing record
61 fights   55 wins   37 knockouts
Olympic gold medal 1960
World Heavyweight Champion 1964–1967, 1974–1978, 1978–1979

Bobby Charlton
(Part one)

Bobby Charlton is one of the most famous footballers ever.

This is the story of his career.

Bobby Charlton was born in Northumberland in 1937. He came from a coal-mining family.

Bobby's grandfather and three of his uncles were footballers.

Bobby's mother Cissie was a football fanatic. She taught Bobby and his brother Jack to play.

Bobby loved going to Newcastle United's ground to see famous players.
Stanley Matthews was his favourite.
Matthews was famous for his speed off the mark. Bobby wanted to be able to play like Matthews so he practised sprinting with his grandfather.

Continued on page 28

Laird Hamilton

Laird Hamilton is the greatest big wave surfer of all time.

He has surfed the world's biggest waves. He surfs 11-metre-high waves and rides at speeds of up to 50 mph.

Laird began surfing when he was two. His stepfather was also a famous surfer. His name was Bill Hamilton.

Laird trains by carrying huge rocks under water.

He rides up hills with 22-kilogram weights on his mountain bike.

Surfer stats

Height: 1.9 metres (6 feet 3 inches)

Weight: 97 kilograms (215 pounds)

Lance Armstrong

Lance Armstrong is the fastest man on two wheels.

Lance got his first bicycle when he was seven years old. As a teenager, he competed in **triathlon** events.

He won the World Road Race Championship in 1993.

By 1996 he was the world's number-one cyclist. Then he found out he had cancer.

He was given a less than 50% chance to live.

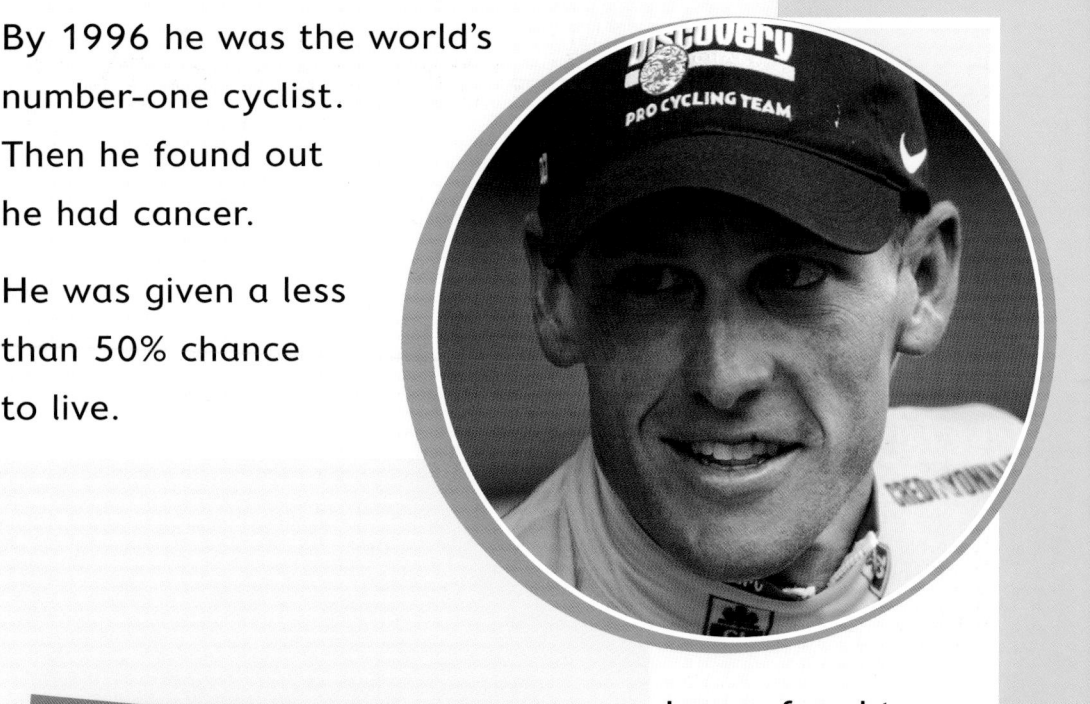

Lance fought back to win the Tour de France seven times in a row.

Ayrton Senna

Ayrton Senna was a famous racing driver.
He was born in Brazil in 1960.

Senna began kart racing when
he was four years old. He won
his first competition at 13.
He went on to single-seat racing,
then **Formula One**.

Senna drove for McLaren from 1988 to 1993. He won three World Championships.

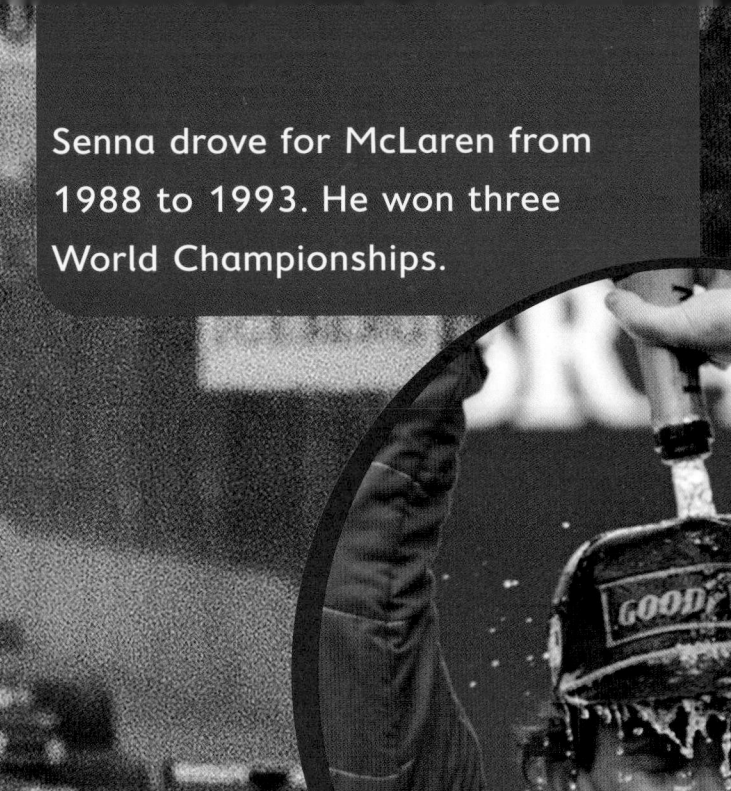

Race record

World Championship titles: 3	
Grand Prix wins: 41	
Pole positions: 65	

Senna changed to the Williams team in 1994. He died in a crash at the San Marino Grand Prix in the same year. He was 34.

Ellen MacArthur

Ellen MacArthur is the fastest person
to sail **solo** non-stop around the world.

Ellen first went sailing on her aunt's
boat when she was six years old.
As a teenager, she saved her school
dinner money to buy her own boat.
She sailed solo around Britain when
she was 18.

Ellen's record

27,354 miles

71 days, 14 hours, 18 minutes

Ellen broke the world record in her boat B&Q in 2005. On her journey, she faced high seas, gales, icebergs and whales!

She was made a Dame in the same year.

Bobby Charlton
(Part two)

In 1953, Bobby was chosen to play for
England Schoolboys. People began to hear
how good he was. Eighteen **scouts** from
leading clubs came to watch him play. They
all offered him deals to sign for their club.

In 1956 Bobby decided to sign for
Manchester United. Their manager was Matt
Busby. Bobby scored twice in his first match.

In 1958, disaster struck. It was a snowy day in February. The team had been playing in the European Cup. Their plane stopped at Munich to refuel. It crashed on take off and caught fire.

Eight young players in the Manchester United squad were killed. Bobby escaped the plane crash with cuts to his head.

Continued on page 36

Red Rum

Red Rum was a famous racehorse.

He was trained in the sea and
on the sands at Southport.

Race record

Trainer: Ginger McCain

Owner: Noel Le Mare

Nickname: Rummie

Grand National wins: 1973, 1974, 1977
Runner-up: 1975, 1976

Lester Piggott was one of 24 jockeys to ride Red Rum.

Red Rum is buried by the winning post at the Aintree race course.

Torvill and Dean

Jayne Torvill and Christopher Dean are world-famous British ice dancers.

They both began ice skating as children. They first skated together in 1975.

They went on to become British, European and Olympic champions.

Torvill and Dean won a gold medal at the 1984 **Olympics**. They got the highest scores ever for figure skating.

Torvill and Dean retired in 1998 and each received an OBE.

Championships

British National Champions: 1980	
European Champions: 1981, 1982, 1984, 1994	
World Champions: 1981–1984	

Steve Redgrave

Steve Redgrave is the world's best rower.
He is also Britain's top Olympian.

Steve got interested in sport during
the **Olympics** in 1972.

He took up rowing at school when he was 13.
He always said he hated training!

Steve won five gold medals in
the **Olympics** from 1994 to 2000.

Steve has also won nine World Championship gold medals. He rowed his way into the record books at the Sydney Olympics in 2000.

He became Sir Steve Redgrave in 2001.

Race times
Race: coxless fours
Winning time: 5:56:24 seconds
Margin of win: 0.38 seconds

Bobby Charlton
(Part three)

Three months after the plane crash, Manchester United reached the FA Cup Final.

They were beaten 2–1 by Bolton, but everyone admired the team's bravery.

In the same year, Bobby played his first match for England. He was to win a record 106 **caps** with the squad.

In 1962, United got to the final of the FA Cup again. They were playing against Leicester.

United won 3–1. Bobby set up the second goal with an amazing flying kick.

Bobby stayed with Manchester United for almost all his career.

When he retired in 1973, he had played in 751 games and scored 245 goals for the club.

Bobby Charlton received a CBE in 1974 and became Sir Bobby in 1994. He has been named Football Writer's Player of the Year.

In 2002, there was a poll to choose the top British sporting legend. Sir Bobby came second, after Sir Steve Redgrave.

Bobby was famous for his 'hair style' well before Beckham!

It has been said that in the 1960s, children around the world knew two words in English: 'Bobby' and 'Charlton'!

Career of a legend
England caps: 106
England goals: 49
World Cup 1966
European Cup 1968
FA Cup 1963
League Division Winners 1957, 1965 and 1967

Great sporting moments

Some sporting events become legends.

Golfer Tiger Woods won his first US **Masters** in 1997. He became the youngest-ever Masters Champion. He set a new Masters best of 271. He won by a record 12 shots.

Muhammad Ali won back the World Heavyweight Championship in 1974. He beat George Foreman. Foreman was six years younger than Ali and he had won his last 40 fights.

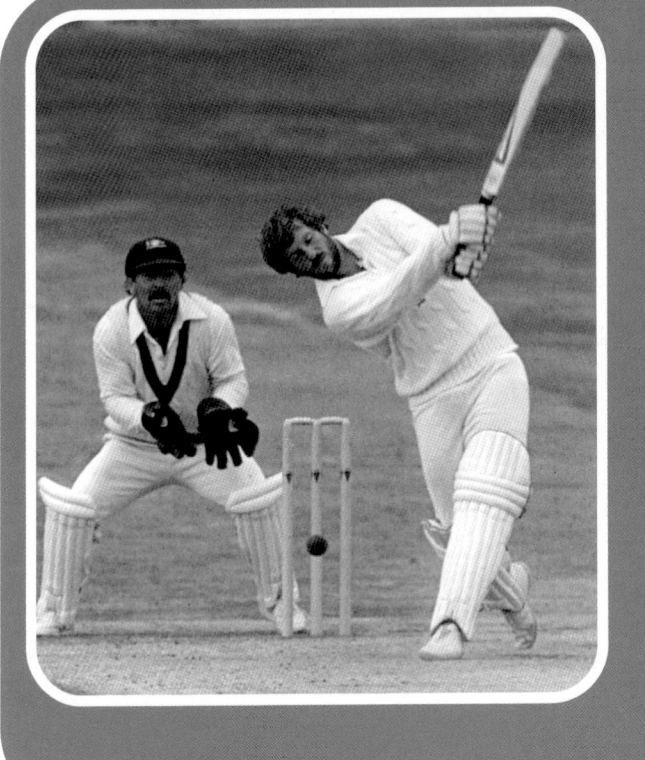

In the 1981 Ashes, England were losing badly at Headingley. The team had even checked out of their hotel! Then Botham came in and got 149 not out. Australia had to bat again. Bob Willis bowled 8 for 43 and England won by 18 runs.

Top five most memorable sporting moments of the 20th century
England win the 1966 World Cup
Ian Botham's 1981 Headingley Test
Steve Redgrave's five Olympic golds
England's 5–1 win over Germany in World Cup qualifier
Ali versus Foreman ('The Rumble in the Jungle')

Source: **Radio Five Live Poll**

Cups and trophies

Some cups and **trophies** are sporting legends.

Trophy	Title	Fact
The Ashes 	Winner of cricket series between England and Australia	The Ashes got its name when Australia had beaten England in 1882. A reporter wrote that English cricket had died. He said its ashes would go to Australia.
The Venus Rosewater Dish 	Winner of the Ladies' Singles title at the **Wimbledon** Tennis Tournament	The silver tray was first presented in 1886. The winner keeps a small copy.

Trophy	Title	Fact
FIFA's World Cup 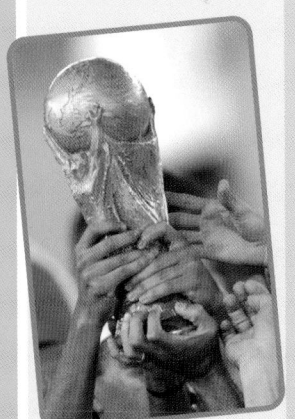	Winner of the Football World Cup	The World Cup is a gold statue of Nike, Greek goddess of victory. It weighs five kilograms. It has the names of the winning teams on the base.
The Yellow Jersey 	Winner of the Tour de France	The yellow jersey is worn by the race leader. 'L'Auto' is the sports newspaper that began the event in 1903. It was printed on yellow paper.

Quiz

1 Which cricket player had the nickname
'the Doctor' and why?

2 Who first ran a mile in less than four minutes?

3 Who was named FIFA's Player of the Century?

4 Where was the 1966 World Cup final played?

5 What was Muhammad Ali's birth name?

6 What was Dame Ellen MacArthur's record-winning
boat called?

7 Where is Red Rum buried?

8 Who is Britain's top Olympian?

9 Who receives the Venus Rosewater Dish trophy?

10 What does the World Cup trophy represent?

Glossary of terms

caps	Appearances representing a team.
GP	A doctor (stands for General Practitioner).
Grand Slam	The world's top tennis tournaments, including Wimbledon, the Australian Open, the US Open and the French Open.
FIFA	The International Football Federation.
Formula One	A motorsport championship.
hat trick	(In football) Three goals scored by one player in a single match.
Masters	Golf championship held in Augusta, Georgia USA.
Olympics	International games held every four years.
pole positions	Front place on the grid or starting positions in a Grand Prix.
scout	Someone who searches for new talent.
solo	Alone, single-handed.
triathlon	A contest in three different events or sports.
trophy	A prize awarded to a winner.
Wimbledon	The Lawn Tennis Association championship.
wit	Clever way of speaking.

More resources

Books

Muhammad Ali: Sports Heroes and Legends
Carrie Golus
Published by Lerner Publishing Group (ISBN 978-0822559603)

**Nudes and Nikes: Champions and Legends of the
First Olympics**
Dyan Blacklock
Allen & Unwin (ISBN 978-1864484557)

Magazines

Ace Tennis Magazine Tennis GB
Interviews with tennis stars and celebrities and stories behind
the world's top tennis tournaments.

Champions Haymarket Publishing Ltd.
The official magazine for the UEFA championships, with match
reports and features on star players.

Cycle Sport IPC Media
Magazine for fans of professional road racing, with inside stories
from the races and interviews with the stars.

Websites

www.bbc.co.uk/schools/ancientgreece/classics/olympics
A lively guide with Flash Player on the history of the Olympics.

www.bbc.co.uk/cbbc/sport
The CBBC sports website with features on stars past and
present.

www.sporting-heroes.net
A photo gallery of sporting heroes with links to sports including
football, cricket and tennis, and information on national and
world records.

DVDs

Manchester United – Legends (2006)
2 Entertain Video (Cat no. ASIN B000BNEMI5HE)

Lance Armstrong – 7 in a Row (2005)
Green Umbrella Productions (Cat no. ASIN B000BNT9A8)

Answers

1 W.G. Grace, because he trained as a GP

2 Sir Roger Bannister

3 Pelé

4 Wembley

5 Cassius Clay

6 B&Q

7 By the winning post at Aintree race course

8 Sir Steve Redgrave

9 The winner of the Ladies' Singles title at the Wimbledon Tennis tournament

10 Nike, Greek goddess of victory

Index